UNDER THE LEADERSHIP of U.S. EPA Administrator Lisa Jackson and "energy czar" Carol Browner, the Obama administration continues to develop an unprecedented amount of new draconian environmental regulations that will severely damage America's beleaguered industrial sector. The scope of these initiatives is breathtaking, going well beyond anything that has ever been attempted in the name of ecological purity in America. While many of us share a sense of foreboding about what the EPA has been doing, few really understand the issues. After all, cap and trade is dead, is it not? With that job-killing, economically disastrous idea out of the way, most people seem to believe that the EPA's ability to interfere with the free market in general and with industry in particular will remain pretty much the same as ever: an expensive annoyance to be sure, but a manageable annoyance nonetheless.

Unfortunately, the hard reality of the situation today is very different and far from encouraging. Cap and trade may be dead, but

that doesn't mean that the EPA and other governmental entities aren't pursuing other ways to sabotage America's ability to use cheap, abundant fossil fuels in order to generate power, which is a vital component of fueling economic recovery. The fact is that the Obama administration and its liberal allies are conducting a full-scale assault on America's energy sector, and on our industrial base, in the guise of environmental protection.

Environmental Protection in America: A Brief History

If we are going to fairly consider where America is today with regard to protecting the environment, we must start with an evaluation of where we have been. Forty years ago, President Richard Nixon signed into law the two landmark statutes that were designed to reverse decades of environmental damage that built up in the industrialized era: the Clean Air Act and the Clean Water Act. Few people, regardless of their ideological bent, could argue against the need for either piece of legislation. People who lived in or near large urban centers could see firsthand how dirty the air was. The evidence ranged from the unnatural color of the sky to the coating of dust that would appear on automobiles parked in the city overnight. Burning rivers and dead lakes testified to the fact that numerous waterways were as dirty as the air.

The Clean Air and Clean Water acts were designed to clean up the mess we had made. At the time they were passed, environmental advocates set reasonable, achievable goals. First, the EPA set up numeric standards for pollutants in the air and water. These were the targets. For example, air would be considered "clean" only if no more than *X* parts per million of particulate matter and *Y* parts per million of carbon monoxide were detected. A similar but more complex scheme was used to define clean water, depending on how the water would be used. Having set these goals, the EPA, along with various state and local regulatory authorities, then started building the regulatory structure that would allow the nation to reach those targets. New standards forced automobile manufacturers to install pollution-control devices on vehicles; oil refineries to introduce new fuel blends; and thousands of factories and power plants to install expensive pollution-control devices.

Business owners grumbled, of course, wondering if the expense was necessary and whether the added costs would put American manufacturers at more of a competitive disadvantage relative to foreign competitors. But ultimately, everyone did what they had to do. Americans paid a little more for their automobiles, power, and a host of products, but the expense wasn't enough to really catch anyone's attention, much less to cause concern. Business owners learned that they had to add a new line item on the expense side of the ledger labeled "Environmental Compliance," and while new expenses are never welcome, this one turned out to be manageable in the broad scheme of things.

The results were astounding. The amount

of particulate matter (that's dust, to you and me) and lead in the air quickly decreased almost a hundredfold. Concentration of other air pollutants, such as carbon monoxide and ozone, dropped precipitously. Fish returned to waterways that had been horribly polluted just a few years before. Lake Erie rose from the dead to become a sportsman's paradise.

But there was another side to the amazing, and amazingly rapid, success stories called the Clean Air Act and the Clean Water Act. Meeting the requirements of both pieces of legislation required a new kind of support infrastructure, and what we have come to call "green jobs" were born. This included everything from the Sierra Club lobbyist pushing Congress to pass more legislation, to the company that makes state-of-the-art pollution-control devices, to the armies of federal, state, and local bureaucrats who make sure that everyone follows the rules. Law firms sprouted environmental departments to help companies that ran afoul of the EPA, and consultants (like me) began to earn a living by guiding businesses through the tangle of regulations that grew more confusing each year.

As is always the case, once you build up a multifaceted industry like the environmental industry, it's extremely difficult to tear it down or even shrink it a little. This is particularly true when government alone has the power to

---

Once you build up a multifaceted industry like the environmental industry, it's extremely difficult to tear it down or even shrink it a little.

---

reduce the size of an industry that – like any service industry – does nothing to create wealth but instead saps capital generated by wealth creators. Absent government mandates, the environmental industry would be a fraction of the size that it is today, for there are few free-market forces that would support such an industry.

And thus we come to the essential conundrum that dominates the increasingly schizophrenic nature of the EPA and environmental policy in this country. On one hand, every administration is anxious to establish its environmental bona fides and trumpet its green triumphs. The agency, likewise, wants everyone to know that it is using taxpayer dollars wisely and is thoroughly protecting the environment. However, nobody is going to declare victory and go home. Nobody is going to say, "That's clean enough, America – let's cut back the size of the EPA and the environmental industry and just go into a maintenance mode." Admitting that we've finished the job, in any facet of environmental protection, would mean that great swaths of the environmental industry would go out of business, from the big companies that produce pollution-abatement equipment to the environmental advocacy groups that provided those companies with a reason to exist. Thus, we have the Zeno's paradox version of environmental policy in America today: We can approach the target of a green planet by halves, but we're not allowed to actually get there.

Thus, even though the goals of the original Clean Air and Clean Water acts have long been fulfilled just about everywhere, those achievements didn't represent an end but rather a beginning. Congress drew up legislation to address other environmental concerns. Bills were passed that aimed to clean up old, poorly managed hazardous-waste dumps (the Comprehensive Environmental Response, Compensation, and Liability Act, also known as "Superfund"); better manage hazardous-waste generation and disposal (the Resource Conservation and Recovery Act); better manage toxic chemicals (the Toxic Substances Control Act); enhance community safety (the Emergency Planning and Community Right-to-Know Act) and do a host of other good things in the name of environmental protection and to enhance our quality of life. There is little doubt that many of these measures were justified, even if the environmental activists usually employed a healthy dose of hyperbole to make manageable problems sound like we were near the end of the world as we know it.

But as more and more environmental legislation was passed, the environmental industry grew larger and larger. The EPA used the authority that Congress granted it to keep environmental goals moving, raising the bar whenever a particular goal was met. Consider ozone, for example.

While ozone is a good thing when it's high in the atmosphere, protecting us from the harmful portion of the sun's rays, ozone is not so welcome at the ground level, where people can breathe it in. Ground-level ozone is commonly called smog and is the primary component of the orange-hued haze that one sometimes sees when flying into a big city on a hot summer day. The original ozone target in the first Clean Air Act was a concentration of 120 parts per billion (ppb) in the air. In other words, if cities controlled air pollution well enough to reduce ozone in the ambient air to 120 ppb or less, then the EPA would define the air as clean – at least with respect to smog.

Around the mid-1990s, it became obvious that just about every metropolitan area, except those located in Southern California, was going to meet the 120 ppb standard. (Southern California is a special and virtually unsolvable case because of the region's geography and weather.) What to do? The Sierra Club and the American Lung Association, along with other environmental groups, pushed for a new lower ozone standard, 80 ppb, and the EPA under the Clinton administration agreed. (That "averaging period" was also changed during the Clinton administration. Ozone concentrations used to be averaged over a one-hour period, but following this change, they have been averaged over an eight-hour period.) More emissions reductions were made, and it became clear that this standard would be met as well. So in 2008 the EPA under the Bush administration lowered the standard again, this time to 75 ppb.

In other words, it doesn't matter whether a Republican or a Democrat is living in the White House. The EPA is its own beast with its own agenda. A particular administration may influence how aggressive the EPA is in cracking down on violations of EPA rules, but the agency's rule-making and standards-setting machinery continues to chug along, no matter who is in charge. For 39 years, from 1970, when the original Clean Air and Clean Water acts were passed, until the end of the Bush administration in 2009, that machinery generated new standards and rules at a fairly consistent, predictable rate. Then Barack Obama took the oath of office, and virtually everything about environmental regulation in America changed.

A Radical Shift at the EPA

Things changed at the EPA when Barack Obama took office and named Lisa Jackson EPA administrator and Carol Browner energy czar. The agency could never be described as a friend to industry, but before Jackson, there were voices within the bureaucracy who listened to the industry side, who understood that evaluating risks vs. rewards should include consideration of economic issues, and who served to check some of the more radical voices within the agency. Under Jackson, the craziest tree-hugging inmates of the EPA are now effectively, if not officially, in charge of the asylum. As a result, the EPA has radically changed course. Rather than increasing the regulatory burden and tightening down on standards at a measured pace (whether or not such actions were actually needed), Lisa Jackson's EPA has shifted the agency into hyperdrive. The EPA has never before used its authority to make and propose anything that comes close to the kinds of sweeping, radical changes in environmental regulation that we have seen in the past two years.

It was, I suppose, inevitable that this would happen. According to popular leftist mythology, George W. Bush was an awful president as far as the environment was concerned.

There's not a bit of truth to that statement. Under Bush, the air, water, and soil continued to get cleaner than it was under Clinton, just as the air, water, and soil was cleaner under Clinton than it was under George H. W. Bush, and so on. Environmental activists didn't like Bush because 1) he was a Republican; and 2) he didn't sue as many "evil" corporations for violations of obscure requirements of environmental regulations as did his predecessor. Whenever George W. Bush's EPA proposed a change in a regulation or standard that would reduce pollution, environmental groups would complain that he didn't go far enough. Sure,

---

It doesn't matter whether a Republican or a Democrat is living in the White House. The EPA is its own beast with its own agenda.

---

the EPA under Bush published rules to reduce mercury emissions from power plants, for example, but he should have reduced them even more. That complaint, when translated by the technically challenged mainstream media, then morphed into the claim that Bush supported an "increase" in mercury emissions in order to protect his buddies in the power industry.

It was all hooey – politically motivated propaganda with no basis in actual fact. But because few people have the time to understand the intricate technical details involved in environmental policy and because the mainstream media generally defaults to reporting whatever environmental-advocacy groups believe as truth (since, in the mainstream media's mind, the Sierra Club or the American Lung Association have absolutely no self-interest when it comes to environmental policy), the idea that Republican administrations are "anti-environment" and Democratic administrations are "pro-environment" has become accepted dogma within the halls of the University of Conventional Wisdom. Given the extreme, irrational anger that the Left directed at the last Bush administration, it's no surprise that an administration swept into office on an anti-Bush platform would use its EPA to clearly distinguish itself from its hated predecessor and to help establish its progressive credentials.

There is no way that Barack Obama's EPA could adhere to the same policy of gradual but measured "regulatory creep" in the environmental arena to which George W. Bush, Bill Clinton, George H. W. Bush, Ronald Reagan, Jimmy Carter, Gerald Ford, and Richard Nixon had all subscribed. Barack Obama needed to prove that he was the polar opposite of his predecessor in every way possible. If he couldn't do that by closing Gitmo or by pulling out of Iraq when he said he would, then environmental policy would have to do. That was a place where he could clearly distinguish himself from George W. Bush – and at very little cost. Industry would bitch and moan, but industry always bitched and moaned. Ultimately, they did what they were told to do and America chugged along. Shoot, if Lisa Jackson played it right, they might even be able to convince Americans that environmental regulations actually *created wealth.* America's economy has expanded by leaps and bounds since 1970, when the Clean Air and Clean Water acts were first passed. Why not link the two together? How about this: "What's good for the environment is good for the economy!" That slogan has a fine ring to it, especially when the unemployment rate is hovering near 10 percent.

And so Barack Obama's EPA has become the darling of the environmental left this side of ecoterrorist groups like Earth First. The policies, regulations, and initiatives that Lisa Jackson's EPA have created guarantee that all facets of the environmental industry will continue to grow for decades to come. And yet there is a caveat that goes with that statement. The only way that all facets of the environmental industry will continue to grow for decades to come is if the wealth-creating portions of America's economy continue to grow and prosper, as well. No service industry like the environmental industry can survive unless the wealth creators who pay them remain profitable. One cannot, for example, continue to enjoy the largesse of energy companies – either in terms of consulting fees or eco-contributions – if those companies disappear as the result of excessive, economically destructive regulations. Have we now crossed that line under the current administration? More and more evidence suggests that we have indeed.

An Unparalleled Record of Extremism

Under the leadership of Lisa Jackson and with the encouragement and support of Obama's ultra-leftist energy czar Carol Browner (a former EPA administrator who in January 2011 resigned her position), the EPA has now tossed aside any pretense of steering a middle course. Remember that, as we have seen, the agency never actually steered anything approaching a middle course when it came to balancing the interests of the environment and the economy, but it was near enough to the middle to avoid catastrophic damage. The economy grew, and America prospered in spite of – not because of, as Lisa Jackson would have us believe – the added burdens that increasingly puritanical environmental regulations place upon the nation's wealth creators.

Rather than balancing the interests of the economic health of the nation against the notion of environmental purity, Lisa Jackson's EPA has gone all in on the latter side of the equation. In justifying the draconian measures

---

Under Jackson, the craziest tree-hugging inmates of the EPA are now effectively, if not officially, in charge of the asylum.

---

proposed by the agency she leads, Jackson has repeatedly said that the EPA cannot legally consider the economic effects of its proposed actions. Under Jackson's leadership, the EPA has abandoned any pretense of considering the advice of the industrial sector in anything but a pro forma way as the agency develops new standards and regulations. Jackson justified the agency's radical change of course because, according to her, the EPA was simply following the "latest scientific advice" available. In turn, the "latest scientific advice" largely consists of studies and opinions authored by committees of the EPA's Science Advisory Board (SAB), an organization established in 1978 that is an artifact of the Carter administration. The SAB and its subordinate committees are – in theory – independent, unbiased scientific working groups that serve as both a check and a balance on the EPA. In fact, the SAB and its committees consist almost entirely of left-wing academic types who, if anything, believe that the EPA isn't nearly aggressive enough when it comes to environmental policy. By deferring to the SAB and its committees, Jackson isn't following the "latest scientific advice" available; rather, she's using the SAB as a convenient excuse to justify an ultra-leftist, neon-green agenda. Let's consider a couple of examples.

Economically Disastrous Revisions of the Ozone Standard

When we briefly reviewed the history of environmental regulation in America, we used the ambient air ozone standard as an example of the way that "regulatory creep" ensures that the EPA, environmental groups, and companies that produce environmental products always have something to do. The first ozone standard was in place for 27 years before it was changed. Then the second ozone standard was superseded by a new one 11 years after that. One of the first actions taken by Lisa Jackson's EPA was to propose reducing the ozone standard yet again, even though the Bush-era standard had not been in place for even a year. And Jackson not only wants to reduce the ozone standard after such a ridiculously short period, but the administrator is also proposing a reduction to ludicrously low levels that will allow the EPA to vastly expand its reach in order to clean up air that has suddenly, by regulatory fiat alone, become "dirty."

Jackson has proposed reducing the current ozone standard of 75 ppb to something between 60 to 70 ppb. (All of these standards are based on eight-hour averages.) In addition, the EPA is proposing a new "secondary standard" that will result in creating more "dirty air" in more areas of the country. Going from 75 ppb to 70 ppb (or less) doesn't seem like much of a change, but even that best-case reduction will have enormous effects on industry and the economy.

See page 22 for a map showing which counties do not currently meet the existing 75 ppb standard.

On page 23 let's take a look at counties that would be out of compliance if the standard is lowered to 60 to 70 ppb.

Counties with Monitors Violating the March 2008 Ground-Level Ozone Standards

0.075 parts per million
(Based on 2006–2008 Air Quality Data)

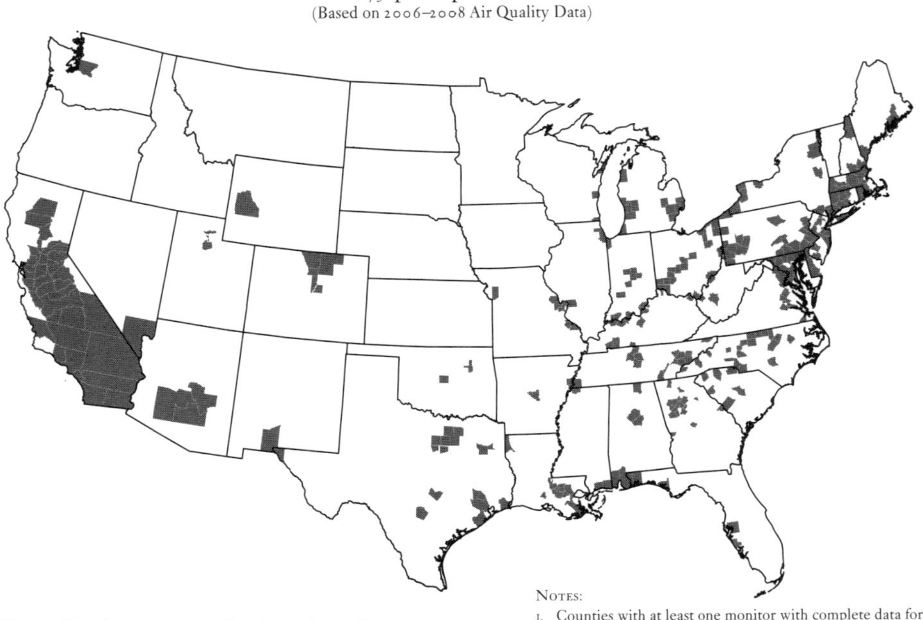

Map provided by USEPA

Counties with Monitors Violating Primary 8-Hour Ground-Level Ozone Standards

0.06–0.070 parts per million

(Based on 2006–2008 Air Quality Data)

EPA *will not* designate areas as nonattainment on these data,
but likely on 2008–2010 data, which are expected to show improved air quality.

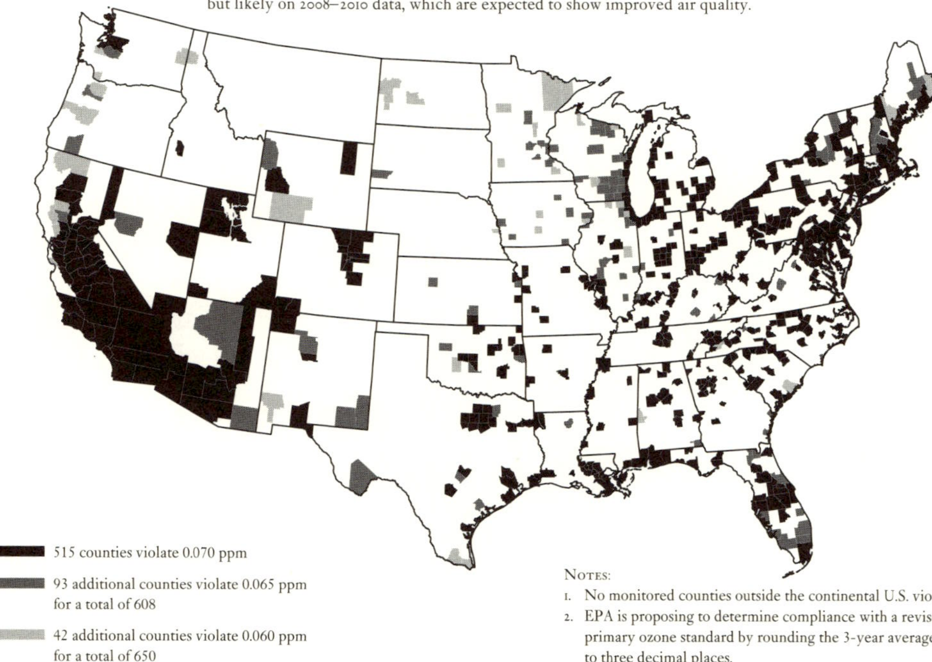

Notes:

1. No monitored counties outside the continental U.S. violate.
2. EPA is proposing to determine compliance with a revised primary ozone standard by rounding the 3-year average to three decimal places.

Map provided by USEPA

The difference between the two maps is striking. Depending on the final standard the agency chooses, the number of counties that don't meet the ozone standard will increase by 60 percent (70 ppb standard) to more than 100 percent (60 ppb standard). For the most part, the counties that don't meet the existing Bush-era standards are large metropolitan areas that are used to managing emissions that form ozone. (Ground-level ozone forms when two pollutants, nitrogen oxides and volatile organic compounds, react with the aid of sunlight on warm days, typically when winds are light and calm.) Big cities sell the low-vapor-pressure gasoline that fights ozone formation in the summer, for example. Many have vehicle-inspection programs in place to ensure that catalytic converters and other pollution-control equipment continue to function properly. Industrial sources in and around big cities are subject to stringent control requirements. Few of these structures exist in the many smaller towns and rural areas that would be affected by the imposition of Jackson's

Barack Obama's EPA has become the darling of the environmental left this side of ecoterrorist groups like Earth First.

draconian standard. The cost of production and the cost of transportation will increase in parts of America that have never felt the heavy hand of the EPA, at a time when the nation can least afford such environmental largesse. As Ted Steichen, policy adviser for the American Petroleum Institute, said during his testimony before Congress regarding the proposed new standard: "To cite a football analogy, EPA is effectively proposing to move the goalposts in the middle of the game. Many local communities will be saddled with new costs that will hurt both large and small businesses and prevent expansion and growth. Fuels that cost more to manufacture would be required in

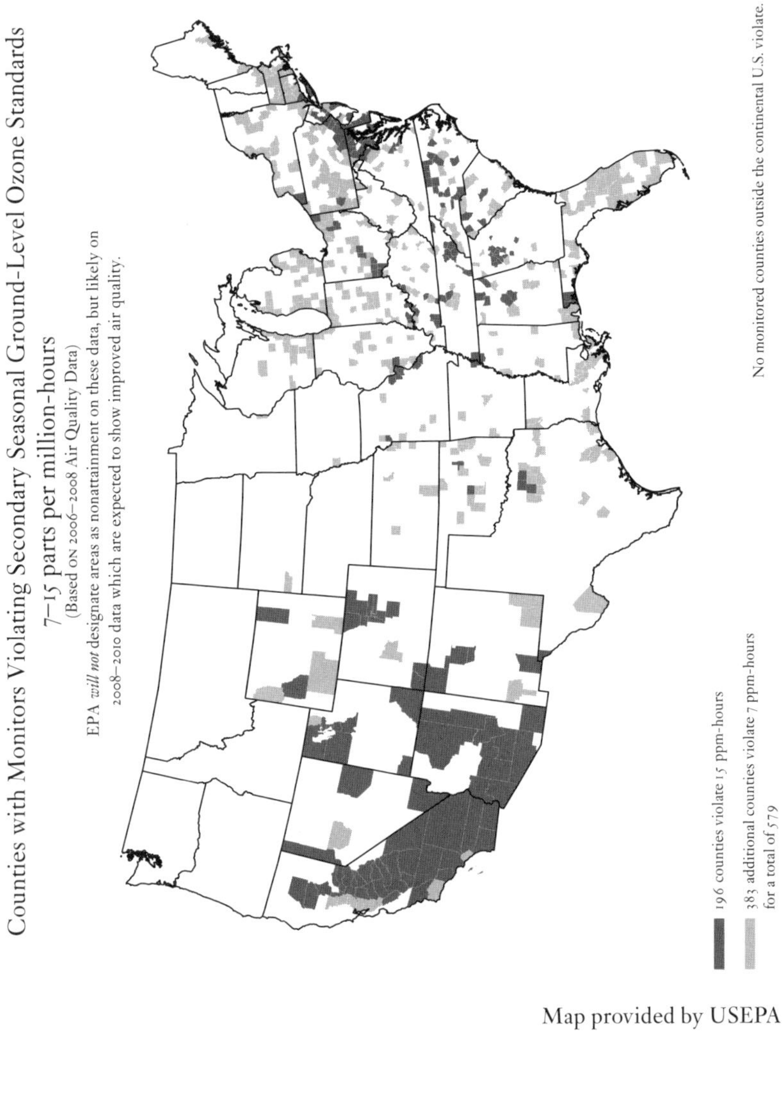

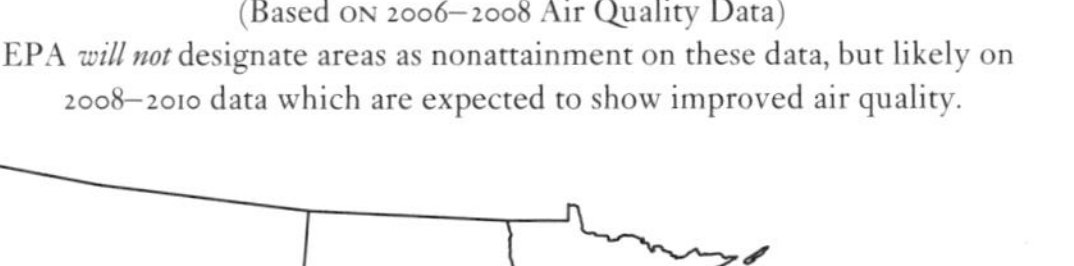

Map provided by USEPA

more areas. Jobs will unnecessarily be lost."

On page 26 take a look at the counties that will be affected by the new secondary ozone standard.

This is not, as the Obama administration hopes you will believe, business as usual in the world of environmental regulation. This is something different, something new and radical and untested. This is a demand (and the agency is making a lot of them) for a level of environmental purity that no nation on earth has ever felt the need to attain before. How can the EPA justify this level of regulation? There are three components to the agency's "green marketing" strategy: minimize, rationalize, and marginalize. Here's how it works:

1) Minimize the Effect – Very few people really understand the technical issues that are at the heart of environmental initiatives, so the agency's party line has been that these new rules aren't really a big deal at all. Without the kind of in-depth analysis that the media just aren't equipped to provide (even if they were of a mind to),

the EPA's assurances that nothing has really changed in the world of environmental regulation will satisfy most people. In a speech marking the 40th anniversary of the Clean Air Act, Jackson defended her agenda and sneered away any suggestions that the agency has radically shifted course. "We can take on the remaining challenges of pollution in our air," she said. "I know because the Clean Air Act took on big challenges – and it worked. We can come together in a collaborative effort, ignore the doomsday exaggerations, and build a common-sense plan together. I know because we've done it before – and it worked."

2) Rationalize the Benefits – The longer our economic woes continue, the more you will hear the following slogan: What's good for the environment is good for the economy. In the course of a few sentences that simply boggle the mind for their absurdity, Jackson tried to link the economic growth that America has experi-

enced during the past four decades to the existence of the Clean Air Act. "And as air pollution has dropped over the last 40 years, our national GDP has risen by 207 percent," she said. "The total benefits of the Clean Air Act amount to more than 40 times the costs of regulation. For every one dollar we have spent, we get more than $40 of benefits in return. Say what you want about EPA's business sense, but we know how to get a return on an investment. In short, the Clean Air Act is one of the most cost-effective things the American people have done for themselves in the last half century."

Where do these amazing economic benefits come from? The rationale that the EPA uses to identify economic savings when it comes to pollution reductions almost always involves one of two areas: fewer worker sick days (and thus increased productivity) and decreased mortality. More about those two issues later on, but as spurious as those overused claims are, they are exceptionally dubious when it comes to Jackson's ozone-standard proposals. The health benefits are linked to a study in which a small number of test subjects showed increased lung capacity when breathing in a few parts per billion less ozone. The increase in lung capacity was small and not really statistically significant, but it was enough for the academics "advising" (read: dictating policy to) the EPA to demand a reduction in the ozone standard. The other common justification for the new ozone standard is the indisputable fact that incidences of asthma are on the rise in the United States. However, no one in the EPA, Sierra Club, or American Lung Association has yet to explain how reducing ozone will help, since we've made drastic reductions in urban ozone concentrations in the past 40 years, while asthma has increased at the same time. If anything, the empirical evidence suggests that we should be pumping more ozone into our breathing air, not less.

3) Marginalize Opposing Voices – In addition to its mandate to protect the environment, the agency's agenda under Jackson includes a new role: guardian of truth. While it is a fact that industry often disagreed with the EPA's actions, industry always had a place at the table when those actions were being considered. The agency generally steered a middle course between the wishes of environmental lobbyists and industry lobbyists, even if it leaned toward the former direction. Today all the industry side gets from the EPA is lip service. The industry side still has a seat at the table – sort of – but nobody at the agency is really interested in what they have to say. Jackson's sneering attitude toward industrial concerns was obvious as she dismissed them in two terse sentences during her Clean Air Act anniversary speech: "Today's forecasts of economic doom are nearly identical – almost word for word – to the doomsday predictions of the last 40 years," she said. "This 'broken

record' continues despite the fact that history has proven the doomsayers wrong again and again."

Is Jackson right? Has environmental regulation been a profit-making enterprise? Or might the converse be true? Could it be that American economic growth occurred despite, not because of, all of the environmental regulation that has sprouted up in the past 40 years? I am reminded of cereal commercials that were popular 30 or so years ago. They would feature an awful sugary cereal in a bowl, surrounded by eggs, oatmeal, orange juice, toast, and a glass of milk. The announcer would then happily announce that the cereal was "part of a complete breakfast." Not really. The cereal was in fact *adjacent* to a complete breakfast. Such is the case when we look at the relationship between environmental regulation and economic growth.

There are many factors that determine where investors will spend their money to build new factories and create new jobs, but it's beyond naive to believe that the environmental regulatory bureaucracy doesn't play a significant role in those decisions. In my own career as an industrial consultant, I've personally witnessed countless examples of investments not made where the decision was ultimately influenced by concerns about environmental costs.

The real cost of the Clean Air Act and other environmental regulations was paid in jobs. Whether Jackson understands it or not, the increased power of the EPA drives jobs away, because that's a big factor when companies choose not to reinvest in existing American factories and when other companies choose not to build new ones here. Of course it's not the only factor – clearly things like labor costs, health care, and OSHA play big roles – but it's an important one. Consider employment data in four industries that were hit hard by environmental regulation: the iron and steel, motor-vehicle, paper, and printing industries:

INDUSTRY SECTOR	TOTAL EMPLOYMENT 1970	1990	2009
Iron and Steel	627,000	276,200	91,200
Motor Vehicles	799,000	812,000	321,900
Paper	700,900	696,700	418,000
Printing	1,104,300	1,569,400	552,200

In addition to losing jobs in industries that once helped form the backbone of our economy, those increases in productivity that the EPA is always talking about cannot be tied to Americans working longer hours because a cleaner environment keeps them healthier. See page 35 for a graph that shows the trend in the length of the work week for the average American worker.

Playing Hardball over Greenhouse Gases

The EPA's claim that it saves billions upon billions of dollars because a cleaner country

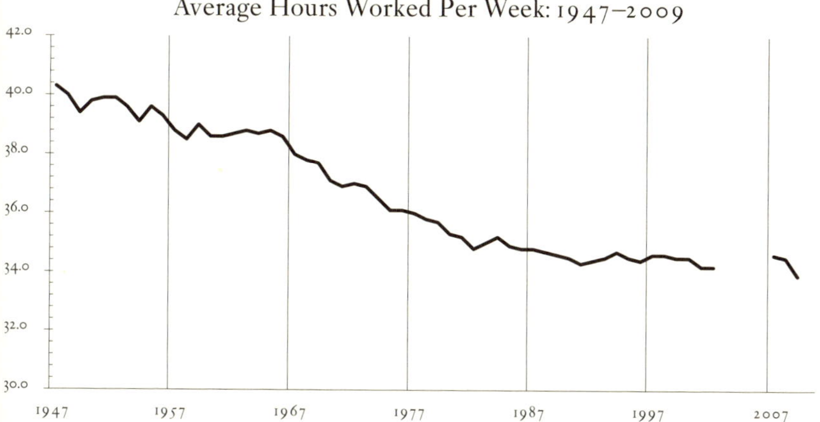

decreases mortality is equally spurious. The reasons that people live longer today involve advances in medicine and health care, not infinitesimal further reductions in pollution. And as we know very well, thanks to America's intense debate about healthcare, our increasingly aging population is increasingly more expensive to care for. Thus the EPA's assertion that increased regulation saves money because Americans live longer is ridiculous on two counts: 1) EPA regulations aren't responsible for increased longevity; and 2) if they were, then those rules would cost people more, not less.

Many people who don't buy into the theory that man-made emissions of greenhouse gases are changing the climate of our planet celebrated when cap and trade was officially declared dead in Congress in 2010. Those celebrations were quite premature. The unfortunate fact is that "global warming" disciples have already put a massive, poorly understood infrastructure in place to limit the nation's use of cheap, abundant fossil fuels,

---

Rather than balancing the interests of the economic health of the nation against the notion of environmental purity, Lisa Jackson's EPA has gone all in on the latter side of the equation.

---

and the EPA is aggressively pursuing a regulatory agenda that will further chip away at America's ability to use homegrown energy resources to fuel economic recovery.

Few realize it, but there is no longer any need for the EPA to regulate greenhouse gases in order to reduce greenhouse-gas emissions in the United States. National greenhouse-gas emissions are down to mid-1990s levels. Some of that reduction is due to economic conditions, but a good deal is the result of state and regional initiatives that require continuing decreases in the amount of fossil fuels burned.

Thirty-three states currently have renewable portfolio standards (RPS) in place. Under these rules, electricity used in the state must be generated using less and less fossil fuel each year. In order to make up the difference, renewable sources that don't emit greenhouse gases must be used in ever increasing percentages. For example, New York's RPS specifies that 24 percent of electricity used in the state has to originate from renewable sources by the year 2013. Illinois's RPS calls for 25 percent renewable generation by 2025. All in all, more than 75 percent of the people in America live in states with RPS programs in place. More are sure to come.

In addition, there are three regional cap-and-trade programs in the United States. East Coast states have banded together under the Regional Greenhouse Gas Initiative, a cap-and-trade program that has been up and running since 2009. West Coast states are developing their own program, called the Western Climate Initiative, while Midwest states are doing the same under the Midwestern Greenhouse Gas Reduction Accord.

The EPA has promulgated new Corporate Average Fuel Economy standards that will reduce greenhouse-gas emissions associated with vehicle emissions. Several EPA initiatives, including drastically reducing ambient air standards for pollutants like ozone, nitrogen dioxide and sulfur dioxide, are backhanded ways of reducing energy use as well. These standards are so stringent that it would be virtually impossible to get approval to build a large source that burns fossil fuel, because such a source would inevitably violate one or more of the standards. Yet in spite of all that has been done to reduce greenhouse-gas emissions in the United States, the agency is bound and determined to use the "command and control" system set forth in the Clean Air Act to reduce them even more.

Rather than going through a formal rule-making process to set standards and specify control strategies for greenhouse emissions, the EPA has decided to rely upon the existing permitting provisions of the Clean Air Act to regulate these emissions, at least in the short term. The EPA began greenhouse-gas regulation on January 2, 2011. It will use a two-phased approach. In Phase One, which will run from January 2, 2011, through June 30, 2011, facilities that would trigger permitting requirements based on their emissions of other (non-greenhouse-gas) pollutants must address greenhouse-gas emissions in the permitting process. (The term the EPA uses for these sources is "anyway sources," meaning that they would have been subject to federal permit requirements "anyway.") In Phase Two, starting on July 1, 2011, any source that is a major source of greenhouse gases must address those emissions when going through the federal permitting processes.

To make greenhouse regulation feasible, the EPA had to figure out a work-around to avoid existing permitting thresholds: 250 tons per year for construction permits and 100 tons per year for operating permits. A relatively small commercial establishment – a church or even a large home – could emit 100 tons per year of greenhouse gases. Accordingly, if the EPA stuck to the permitting thresholds specified in the Clean Air Act, the universe of regulated sources would be impossibly large. By the EPA's own admission, sticking to the Clean Air Act in the case of greenhouse gases would inflate the number of operating permits from several thousand to more than 1 million. The regulatory structure could not possibly manage that many permits. Arguably, this is clear evidence that the Clean Air Act was not designed or intended to be used to regulate a "pollutant" such as carbon dioxide and other greenhouse gases. If the nation chooses to limit greenhouse-gas emissions, Congress should pass legislation that defines how that is to be done and delegate authority to the EPA to implement its will. However, the EPA has decided to press forward using its authority under the Clean Air Act, even though a strict interpretation of the act means that the agency will be required to regulate a universe of emissions sources far too large for it to actually regulate.

In order to avoid the problem, the EPA has creatively interpreted the Clean Air Act through the so-called Tailoring Rule. Through the Tailoring Rule, the EPA declared that it can alter the permitting threshold in the case of greenhouse gases. Well, sort of. Clearly anticipating a legal challenge, the EPA retained the 250- and 100-ton-per-year thresholds when it comes to *unmodified* total greenhouse-gas emissions, but it has added another test as part of the formula: the amount of "carbon dioxide equivalent" emissions.

Theoretically, it's not just carbon dioxide that causes global warming. Other chemicals like methane (the primary component of natural gas) can cause global warming too. But, the theoretical global warming "power" of each of these chemicals is somewhat different. A pound of methane in the atmosphere, for example, helps retain about 21 times more heat than a pound of carbon dioxide. In order to get every compound that theoretically causes global warming on the same page, the environmental community uses the term "carbon dioxide equivalent." Basically, you multiply the global warming power (called "global warming potential," or GWP) of each compound to get to the equivalent amount of carbon dioxide that each compound represents. Carbon dioxide equivalent is commonly abbreviated CO_2e. Thus, one ton of methane emissions (with a multiplier of 21) is calculated as 21 tons of CO_2e. The multiplier for nitrous oxide is 310, and the multipliers to get to CO_2e for certain refrigerants are in the thousands.

Whether Jackson understands it or not, the increased power of the EPA drives jobs away.

When a facility calculates its total greenhouse-gas emissions, it does two calculations. The first, as we have seen, is to calculate the total amount of greenhouse-gas emissions without using any multipliers. This total is compared to the 100- and 250-ton-per-year thresholds, but it really doesn't mean anything, because the facility still has to do the CO_2e test. In this test, you apply the multipliers and then add up all of the emissions as CO_2e. Permit requirements kick in only if that total is over 75,000 tons per year for construction permits or 100,000 tons per year for operating permits. This additional test allows the EPA to drastically narrow the universe of regulated greenhouse sources, because this CO_2e threshold is very high. This is the "tailoring" that the agency is using to avoid the absurdity that naturally comes from trying to regulate greenhouse gases under the Clean Air Act.

Having decided that it can force states to exercise permitting authority over greenhouse-gas emissions through the Clean Air Act, the EPA then told the state agencies that issue the permits what standards to use when considering greenhouse-gas emissions controls. In guidance issued in November 2010, the EPA directed state agencies to focus on energy efficiency when evaluating greenhouse-gas control. In order to determine that a facility is operating at optimum energy efficiency, the EPA tells state agencies that they should delve into the design and operational details of proposed projects and that their decisions on such matters should be codified in permit documents. Examples of ways that state agencies are to impose themselves in design and operational decisions include the choice of the type of a boiler, the way that energy is used, the amount and manner in which waste heat is recovered, and the way that parts of a process are maintained and operated.

It's important to note that very few permit writers working in state agencies have the experience or skills to make these kinds of decisions. With few exceptions, most permit writers are recent college graduates or "old-timers" who do not possess the skill sets to flourish in the private sector. Expecting such individuals to impose their will in a process that has heretofore been guided by free-market principles is a recipe for disaster.

As troubling, the EPA has directed state agencies to ignore the issue of manufacturer guarantees when evaluating greenhouse-gas controls. Traditionally, a proposed control technology need not be considered unless the manufacturer of the technology was willing to guarantee a certain level of performance. This sensible policy protected buyers and kept the number of vendors selling the environmental equivalent of snake oil to a minimum. However, the EPA has abandoned this policy when it comes to greenhouse gases. As part of their guidance, the EPA told state agencies that the lack of a performance guarantee is not sufficient reason to reject a proposed control measure. Doubtless, the EPA hopes this will encourage innovative control measures, but it is more likely to generate a host of unworkable, technically flawed "magic solutions" that always seem to spring up when unscrupulous vendors sense a government-mandated opportunity. Industry will no longer be able to ignore such vendors, and state agencies will be in a position to force such vendors' products onto buyers.

In summer 2010, 13 states pushed back and asked the EPA for the three years that the Clean Air Act allows them to revise their regulatory strategies. Known as State Implementation Plans, or SIPs, these plans are the blueprints that state and local agencies use to achieve clean-air goals. The act formalized the idea that the federal agency should define where the nation wanted to be in terms of air quality, but the individual states should be allowed to figure out the best way to get there.

The SIP approval process has been a key feature of the Clean Air Act since that particular piece of legislation was passed. Yet when it comes to greenhouse gases, Lisa Jackson's EPA is demanding that state and local authorities ignore those provisions of the act and submit new SIPs immediately, even though the feds haven't even established definitive emissions targets for greenhouse gases. Essentially, the states have been asked to put their faith in the EPA in the expectation that the feds' decision will ultimately be "the right thing."

Of the 13 states that asked for the time to which they were statutorily entitled before revising their SIPs, only Texas stuck to its guns. In a scathing letter, Texas Attorney General Greg Abbott told Lisa Jackson that the Lone Star State would not "pledge allegiance to the USEPA," thus offering further proof that it's never wise to mess with Texas. In turn, the EPA can be expected to withhold approval of any federal permits that are issued in the state in the future. This is thus a game of chicken on the big stage. Texas is going to press forward with its permit program on the state's own authority, while the feds hope that their refusal to play along will scare away potential developers in one of the nation's few economic bright spots. The outcome of this battle will likely define the future of greenhouse-gas regulation in the United States. If Texas wins, the road to rolling back the enormous and enormously expensive greenhouse-gas-regulation infrastructure that has been put into place will be wide open. If Texas loses, we're in for a very challenging few decades.

The Tip of the Iceberg

We've examined a couple of environmental initiatives in some depth, but we've hardly scratched the surface. Barack Obama's EPA is introducing new regulations at a pace and scope that we have never seen before in virtually every area that the agency touches. The agency is also studying new ways to micromanage America in the name of environmental purity.

There's a working group that's studying new ways to address the pollutants in stormwater runoff, for example. Mind you, new and more stringent stormwater rules were just put in place during the previous administration, but – by definition – nothing that the EPA did while George Bush was president could possibly be good enough for Lisa Jackson. Accordingly, the stormwater working group is

---

If the nation chooses to limit greenhouse-gas emissions, Congress should pass legislation that defines how that is to be done and delegate authority to the EPA to implement its will.

---

considering, among other things, expanded use of the EPA's licensing authority in order to control the manufacture and use of consumer products that might impact stormwater runoff. If that sounds like a stealthy way to introduce more government control into the economy and raise a little revenue to boot, it's probably because that's what it is.

Another task force is considering ways to improve waterway management, including ocean management. This group's activities were the source of the "Obama wants to ban fishing" story that made the rounds in 2010. While the Interagency Ocean Policy Task Force has not been directed to ban sportfishing or even to explore that issue, looking at fishing regulations and policies is most definitely within the task force's scope of work. Is a fishing ban in our future? Almost certainly not. But are additional rules on the way that will affect commercial fishing and, perhaps, sportfishing in some areas? Almost certainly so.

This is the most aggressive EPA that the nation has ever seen. Its tentacles are reaching out into society and the economy in ways that very few members of the public can possibly imagine. We're looking at the tip of a huge iceberg that will affect America for years to come. And, like another famous iceberg, this one has the ability to sink the ship that has been this nation's amazing vessel of prosperity.

First American edition published in 2011 by Encounter Books, an activity of Encounter for Culture and Education, Inc., a nonprofit, tax exempt corporation.
Encounter Books website address: www.encounterbooks.com

Manufactured in the United States and printed on acid-free paper. The paper used in this publication meets the minimum requirements of ANSI/NISO Z39.48–1992 (R 1997) (*Permanence of Paper*).

FIRST AMERICAN EDITION

LIBRARY OF CONGRESS CATALOGING-IN-PUBLICATION DATA

Trzupek, Rich.
How the EPA's green tyranny is stifling America / by Rich Trzupek.
p. cm. — (Encounter broadsides)
ISBN-13: 978-1-59403-588-3 (pbk. : alk. paper)
ISBN-10: 1-59403-588-1 (pbk. : alk. paper)
1. Environmental management—United States. 2. Environmental policy—United States. 3. Environmental protection—United States. 4. United States. Environmental Protection Agency. 5. Obama, Barack. I. Title.
GE310.T788 2011
363.70973—dc22
2011006559

10 9 8 7 6 5 4 3 2 1